LOYISOMKIZEART

KWEZI™

COLLECTOR'S EDITION
ISSUE: 7 - 9

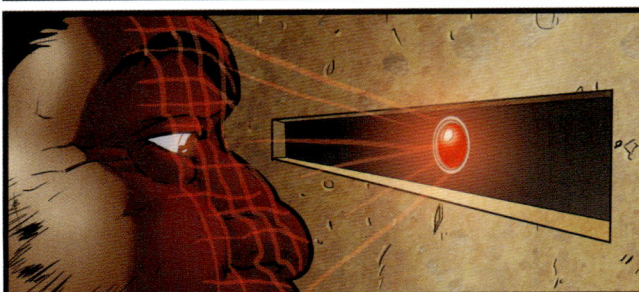

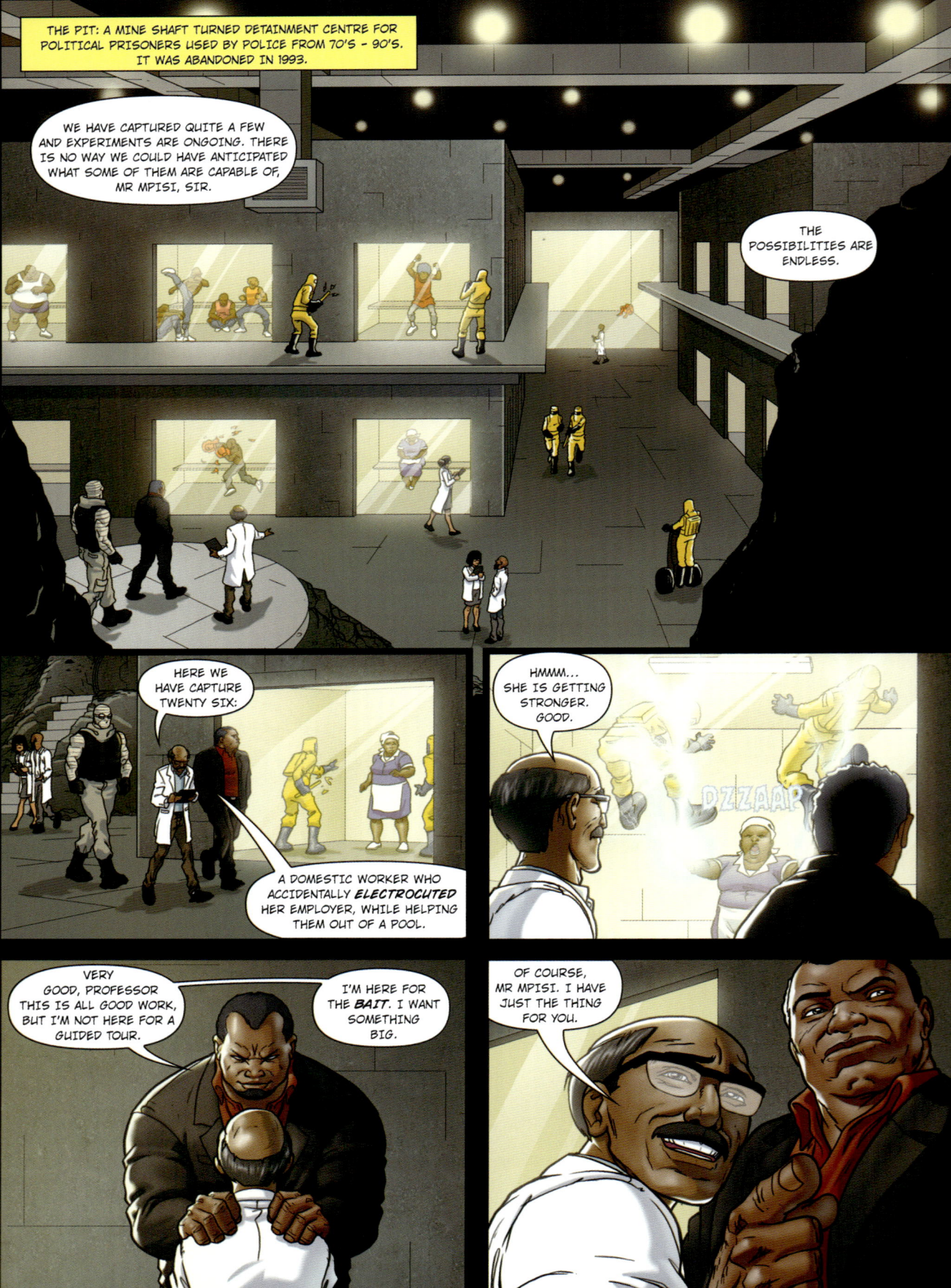

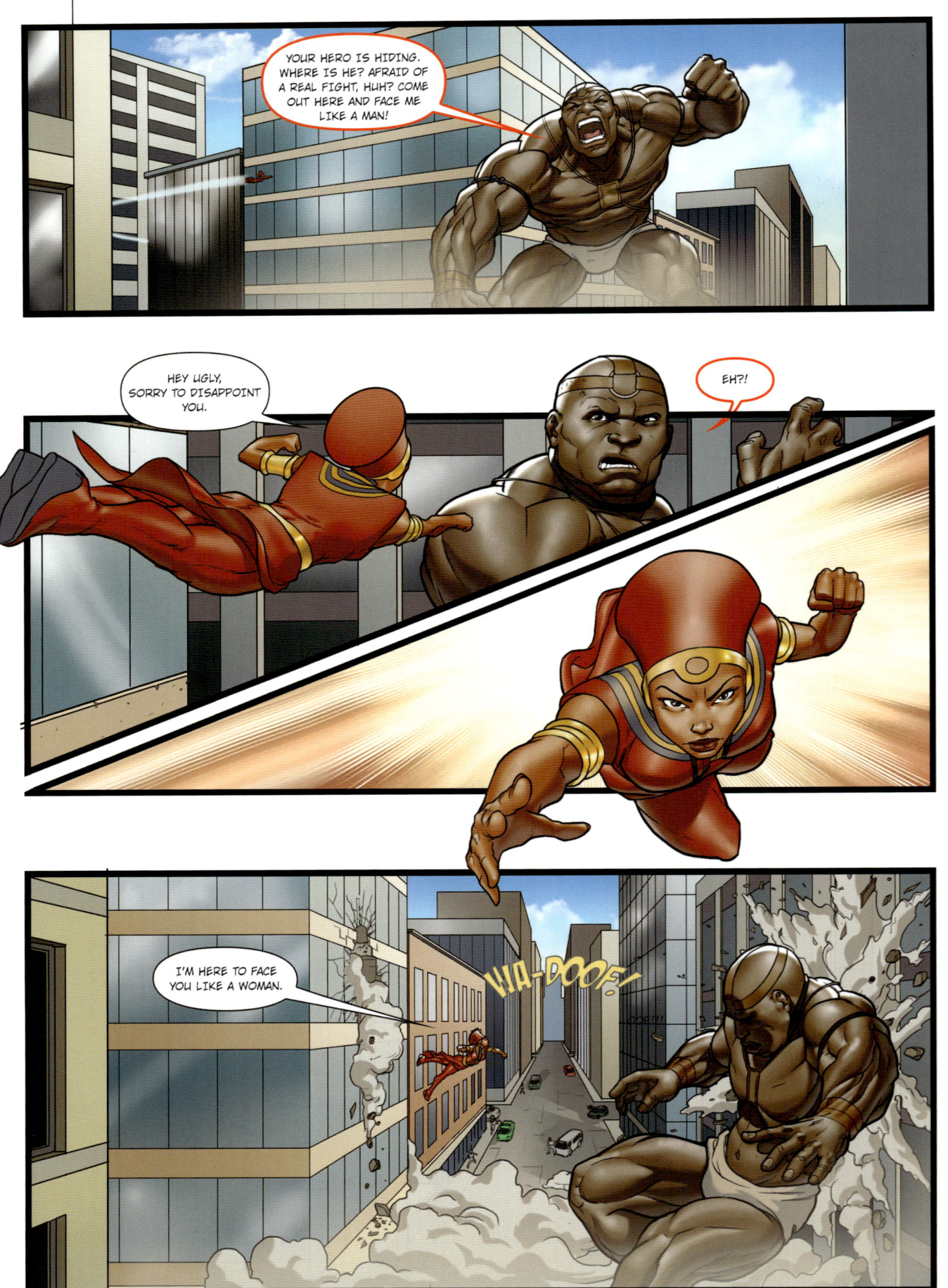

KWEZI
THE PROCESS

1. PENCILS

2. INKS

3. FLAT COLOUR

HEY FANS, HERE'S A SNEAK PEEK INTO THE CREATIVE PROCESS BEHIND THE KWEZI-VERSE.

THE FINAL ARTWORK

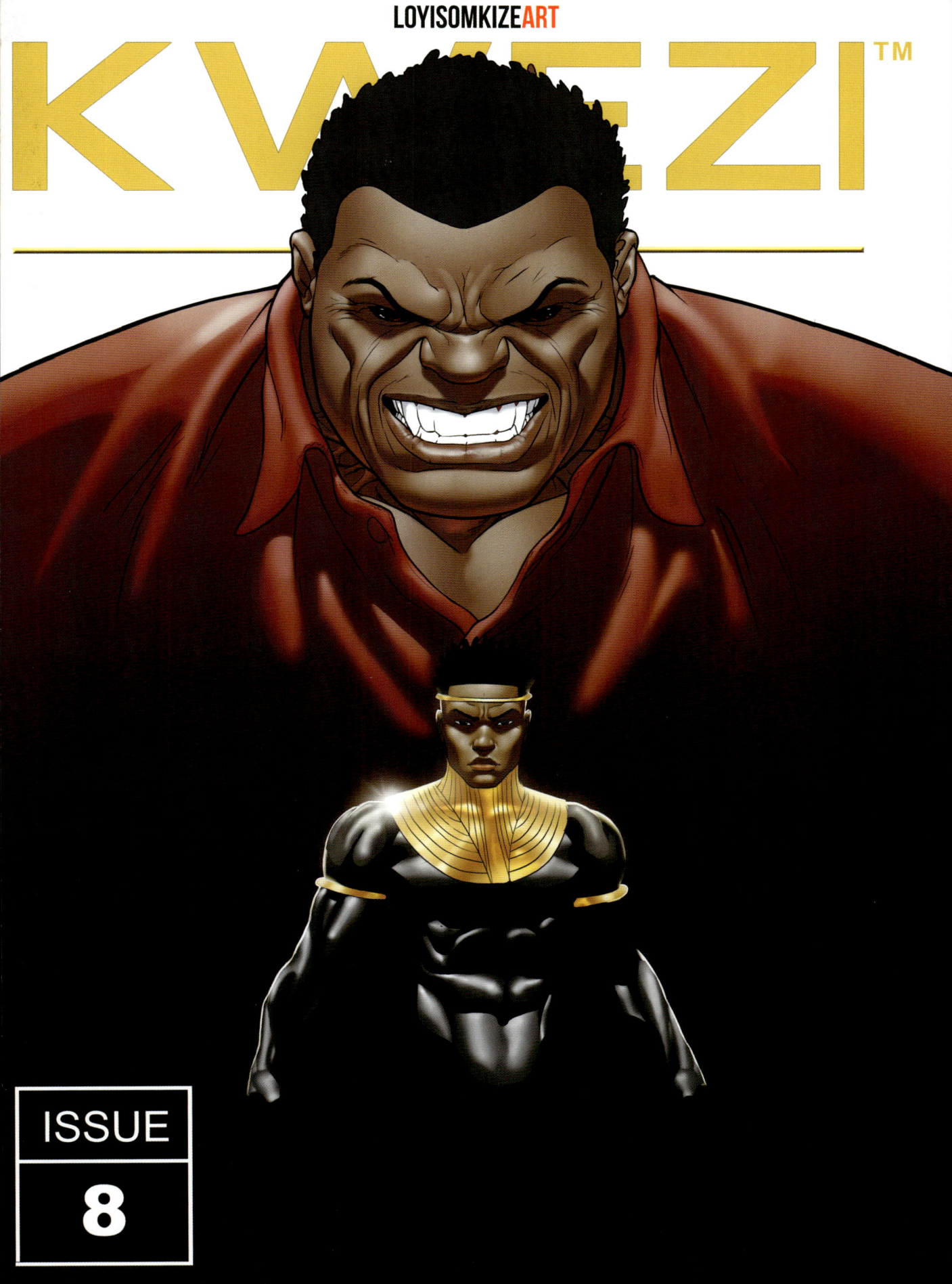

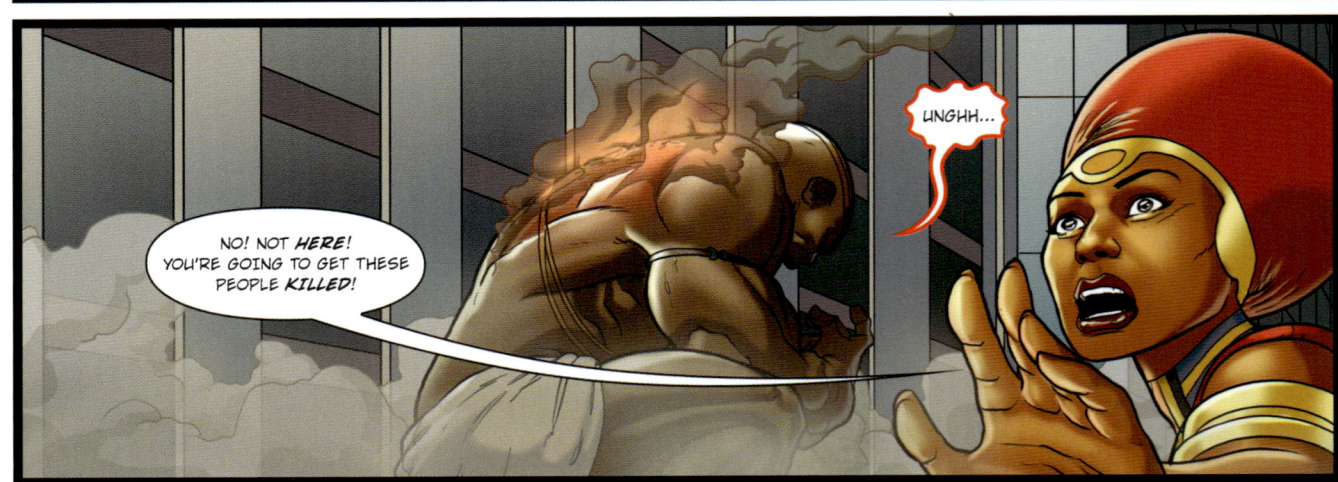

CONCEPT DRAWINGS

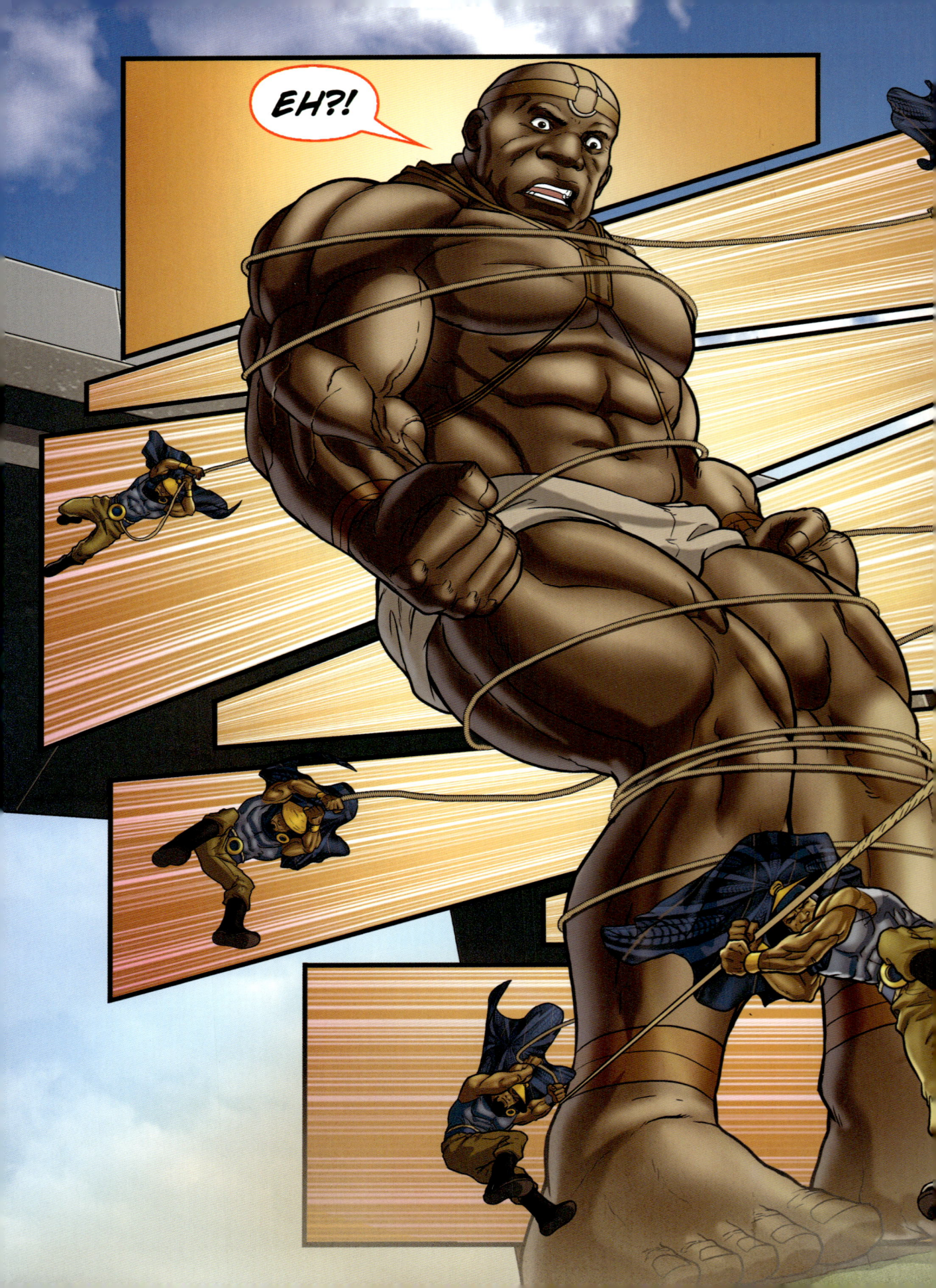

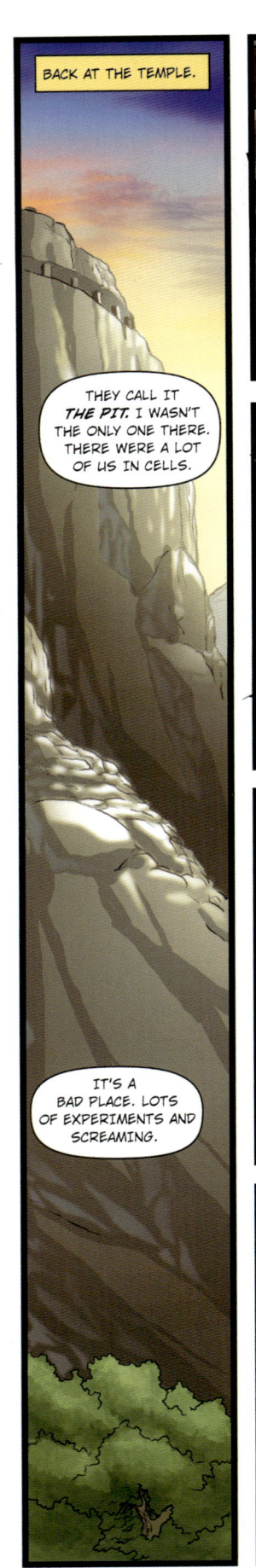